ANTARCTICA
THE GREAT WHITE CONTINENT

by MIRIAM SCHLEIN

illustrated with photographs

HASTINGS HOUSE • PUBLISHERS

New York, N.Y. 10016

ACKNOWLEDGMENTS

The author wishes to thank Dr. Raymond Stross, Division of Biology at the University at Albany and Mr. Guy Guthridge of the National Science Foundation, both of whom read an early draft of this book and offered valuable comments.

She also wishes to thank Mr. Robert A. Carlisle at the Office of Information of the Department of the Navy for his generous cooperation, as well as the personnel at the Naval Photographic Center.

Title page:
Lt. Helmar Hansen of Amundsen's expedition.

Library of Congress Cataloging in Publication Data
Schlein, Miriam.   Antarctica: the great white continent.
  SUMMARY: An introduction to the geography and animal
life of the southernmost continent, 95 percent of
whose surface is covered with ice.
    1. Antarctic regions—Juvenile literature. [1. Antarctic regions] I. Title.
    G863.S34   1979   919.8'9   79-21320 ISBN 0-8038-0482-2

Published simultaneously in Canada by Saunders of Toronto, Ltd., Don Mills, Ontario
Printed in the United States of America

We will use metric terms of measurement, along with the traditional American terms.

Comparing Metric and Regular Measurements

When you know:	you can find:	if you multiply by:
inches	millimeters	25
feet	centimeters	30
yards	meters	0.9
miles	kilometers	1.6
millimeters	inches	0.04
centimeters	inches	0.4
meters	yards	1.1
kilometers	miles	0.6
pounds	kilograms	0.45
kilograms	pounds	2.2

Temperature

When you know:	you can find:	if you:
degrees Fahrenheit	degrees Celsius	subtract 32 from Fahrenheit. Then multiply by 5/9.
degrees Celsius	degrees Fahrenheit	take 9/5 of Celsius. Then add 32.

$F = 9/5\ C + 32$ 0 is freezing on the Celsius scale
$C = 5/9\ F\text{-}32$ 32 is freezing on the Fahrenheit scale

mm stands for millimeter (about 1/25 of one inch)
cm stands for centimeter (a little less than ½ of one inch)
m stands for meter (a few inches more than a yard)
km stands for kilometer (about 6/10 of one mile)
kg stands for kilogram (a little more than two pounds)

About 100,000 years ago, the world got very cold. A large part of the land that is now the United States was covered with mile-thick ice. Only the mountaintops stuck up above the ice.

Scientists do not exactly know why it got so cold. Maybe the sun gave off less heat at that time. Maybe volcanoes erupted and put lots of dust into space which blocked the sun's rays to earth. Or maybe there was a change in the way the earth was moving through space, either in its path circling around the sun, or in the way it spun on its axis. That would have changed the earth's temperature.

About 11,000 years ago, the world warmed up again. It was not the first time this had happened. We do know that at least three times before, the world had gone into a long cold period. This part of the world's history is called The ICE AGE.

We do not know whether the ICE AGE is over. Maybe, in thousands of years, the place where you are right now will again be covered with mile-thick ice.

That is what Antarctica is like today. It is in an Ice Age.

1. Parts of the United States probably looked like this during its glacial periods. (This photo was actually taken recently, in Antarctica.)

2. An outline of the United States, placed on an outline of Antarctica.

It is the coldest place in the world. It is the southernmost place on earth. It is larger than the United States, and about 95% of it is covered with ice. All this ice is called the POLAR ICE SHEET.

Where Did All The Ice Come From?

In some parts of Antarctica, about 60 inches of snow fall in a year—about 150 cm. In other places, less snow falls. But it is so cold there, most of the snow never melts. More snow falls on top of the old snow. Weight and pressure mash it all together. It turns into a solid mass of ice, in some places 3 miles thick (about 5 km).

This ice doesn't melt, but it doesn't just stay there, either. The entire ice sheet moves slowly downward, from high, inland areas. Finally, after thousands of years, it reaches the sea. Even here, it doesn't stop. There are some places where the ice keeps moving out, over the water. It makes an ICE SHELF over the water. In some spots this ICE SHELF is about 1,000 feet thick (about 300 meters).

At last, far out over the sea, big pieces begin to crack off. They become big, flat-topped icebergs that are

6

3. Big drifting pieces that have cracked off the ice shelf are called icebergs.

sometimes 100 miles long (about 160 km). They drift northward, where the ocean is warmer. Here, finally, they break up and melt and become part of the ocean.

The high point of an ice sheet is called the crown, or DOME. There are three domes in Antarctica. At the dome, the ice is thickest and moves very slowly. In a whole year, it may move just a few feet.

Moving downward, the ice forms rivers of ice. Here, it moves faster, sometimes moving about 3 feet (about 1 meter) in just one day. A river of ice like this is called a GLACIER.

4. A river of ice is called a glacier.

How Cold Is It In Antarctica?

Inland, high up on the ice sheet, is the coldest place on earth. In winter (which starts there in June) the temperature is generally between −40° and −70°Celsius. (−40° to−94°Fahrenheit.)

Near the coast, it is not as cold. There, the temperature is between−20° and−30°C. (−4° to−22°F.)

In summer, up on the ice sheet, the temperature is about−20° to−35°C. (−4° to−31°F.) Along the coast, it may go up to about 5°C. (41.F.)

The lowest temperature ever recorded on earth was−88°C. (−126°F.). This was on the Antarctic ice sheet.

5. *Antarctic seasons are the reverse of ours. This is because the earth is tilted at an angle as it goes around the sun. So, when a place north of the equator (like the United States) is tilted toward the sun, a place south of the equator (like Antarctica) is tilted away from the sun.*

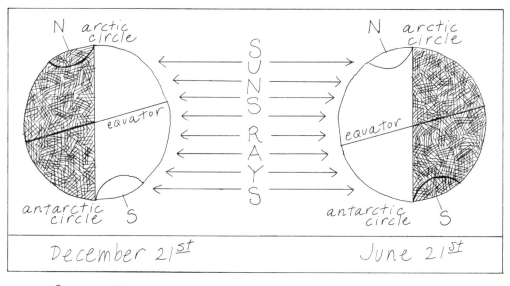

Why Is Antarctica The Coldest Place In The World?

The two "poles"—Antarctica to the south, and the Arctic to the north—are the coldest places on earth. This is because the sun's rays hit them indirectly, at a low angle. But Antarctica is even colder than the Arctic for two reasons:

1. The Antarctic ice sheet covers high mountains, and is at an average of 7,500 feet (about 2,250 meters) above sea level. At high altitudes, the air is colder. The northern Arctic polar region is at sea level. In fact, the North Pole is located right *on* the Arctic Ocean.

2. Antarctica has large inland areas that are far from the warming influence of the oceans.

6. A view of Arctic ice, near the North Pole.

Who Discovered Antarctica?

More than 2,000 years ago, Greek thinkers like Pythagoras and Aristotle believed that the world was round. Since they knew there were cold, frozen lands far up in the north part of the world, they felt that it was logical to assume that there were also cold lands in the southern part of the earth. This would give a kind of balance to the earth.

The cold northern lands they called Arktos, naming it after the star constellation of the Great Bear, seen in the northern skies. So, the unseen frozen southern lands they called anti-arktos, or "opposite arktos." This is how Antarctica got its name.

They put Antarctica on their maps. Even though no one had ever seen it, they felt sure it was there.

In 1772, an expedition set out from England to look for Antarctica. The leader was Captain James Cook.

7. In 1772, Captain Cook set out for Antarctica.

In two small wooden sailing ships, *Resolution* and *Adventure*, they sailed southward. The *Resolution* was only 110 feet long (about 33 meters), and 35 feet (about 10 meters) broad of beam; the *Adventure* was even smaller. On board they carried cattle, sheep and pigs to start breeding herds in the southland.

Cook and his men were the first people ever to cross the Antarctic Circle. No one had ever sailed so far south.

8. *Captain Cook was the first to sail south of the Antarctic Circle, which is shown by the dotted line on this map.*

11

Through iceberg-filled waters, they sailed completely around Antarctica. They sailed for 1,114 days, and traveled 67,500 miles (about 108,000 km). But at no point could Cook get far enough south even to see land. The frozen ice pack kept him back.

Even though Captain Cook could not see Antarctica, he believed it was there. In February, 1775, he wrote in his Journal:

> "I firmly believe there is a tract of land near the Pole, which is the source of all the ice... but the sea is so peskered with Ice that the land is inaccessible." "...a Country doomed by Nature to lie buried under everlasting ice and snow." "...the risk one runs...is so very great...I doubt...if the land...will ever be explored."

Captain Cook was a great explorer, but he was mistaken. In spite of everything, men from many nations did finally get to explore Antarctica, bit by bit.

9. Captain Cook's crew takes on ice for water.

10. *Nathaniel Palmer, a ship's captain at the age of 20, may have been the first person to set eyes on Antarctica.*

The Early Explorers

Nathaniel Palmer was an American from Connecticut. At the age of 20, he was captain of a small sloop, *Hero*, which was only about 47 feet (about 14 meters) long. In 1820, he sailed to Antarctic waters with an American seal-hunting fleet.

It was mid-November—summer in Antarctica. While sailing *Hero* amidst the icebergs, Palmer sighted a stretch of coastline, and recorded its exact position in his log. Some historians believe that this was the first sighting of Antarctica. Others think the first sighting was made by an Englishman named Edward Bransfield.

In 1819, William Smith, captain of an English freighter, sighted snow-covered lands to the south as his ship was going around the tip of South America. The British admiralty assigned Captain Edward Bransfield of the Royal Navy to sail back and investigate. He did, with Captain Smith to guide him.

On January 30th, 1820, Bransfield sighted "two high mountains, covered with snow." He marked their position on his chart. Some historians think Bransfield's was the first mainland sighting. They believe what Palmer saw was the coastline of an island.

There was another explorer who might have really been the first to see the Antarctic continent.

In 1819, Thaddeus von Bellingshausen sailed from Russia with two ships, *Vostok* and *Mirnyi.*

In January, 1820, they crossed the Antarctic Circle. On January 27th, Bellingshausen reported seeing vast ice fields to the south. Some historians feel that he was not looking at a frozen sea of ice, but at the continent itself. This would have made him the first man to see Antarctica.

As Captain Cook had done, the Russians sailed completely around Antarctica. But they were able to get farther south than Cook. They were the first to sight land below the Antarctic Circle. It was a large island, which they named Alexanderland, after the Czar.

Then they sailed on through terrible storms. At times the fog was so thick, the sailors hung down from ropes around the outsides of the ships, so that they could spot icebergs faster, since fog is thinner near the water.

In January, 1821, Bellingshausen wrote this in his diary:

"The center of the continent must be entirely firm, a sheet of ice, added to by snow and hail, and frozen into a solid block..."

That same year John Davis, a Connecticut sealing captain, and his crewmen were probably the first ever to set foot on the mainland of Antarctica, during a search for new sealing grounds.

France was next in sending out a large national expedition to Antarctica. It sailed in 1837, under the command of Admiral Jules Sebastian Cesar Dumont D'Urville.

11. When the fog lifted, Bellinghausen was startled to see Palmer's small ship sailing right beside him. Before this neither had seen the other.

It was D'Urville's goal to find the location of the South Magnetic Pole. This is not the same as the South Pole. The South Pole is the most southerly spot on earth. The South *Magnetic* Pole is the south point to which a compass needle will point. They are not in the same place.

D'Urville sailed along the side of Antarctica south of Australia. Suddenly, his compass needle began to swing back and forth wildly. This showed that they were very close to the magnetic pole. They could not reach the exact spot, because it was inland, and they were not able to land because the shoreline was a high wall of solid ice. D'Urville estimated the position of the South Magnetic Pole.

12. Captain D'Urville's ships, ASTROLABE and ZELÉE.

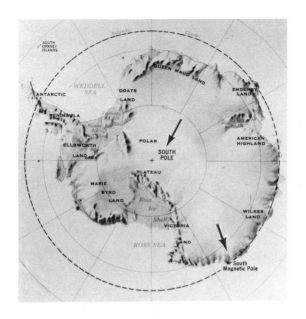

13. The South Magnetic Pole is not in the same place as the South Pole.

Locating the South Magnetic Pole was an important discovery for navigation. We know now that D'Urville's estimate was very close. The South Magnetic Pole is near the Antarctic coastline, south of Sidney, Australia. It is 1,500 miles (about 2,400 km) away from the South Pole.

Bit by bit, Antarctic explorers were beginning to get a good idea of what Antarctica was like. Admiral D'Urville wrote in his diary:

"The continent appears to consist of a formidable layer of ice...which forms the crust over a base of rock."

In 1840, Captain James Ross of the British Royal Navy was also sailing toward Antarctica. Nine years before, Ross had discovered the North Magnetic Pole. Now he wanted to discover the one to the south. On the way, stopping off in Tasmania, Ross heard the news that Admiral D'Urville had already done so.

Ross then changed his plans. His ships, *Erebus* and *Terror,* had been specially rebuilt for the Antarctic voyage, with double-decks, and a layer of copper to protect the keel against the ice. Knowing this, Ross dared something no one had ever tried before. He smashed right through the frozen pack-ice and sailed through open water along the coast where no one had ever sailed before.

One morning, Ross saw something that amazed him. He saw smoke and flames shooting up from an Antarctic volcano. He named it Mount Erebus, after his ship.

Because the shoreline was a tall cliff of ice, Ross could not land on the mainland. So he raised the Union Jack on a small offshore island, and named that part of Antarctica Victorialand, in honor of Queen Victoria. Ross also discovered the ice shelf which is now named after him.

14. Captain James Ross of the British Royal Navy. The Ross Ice Shelf is named after him.

15. A recent photo of Mt. Erebus. It is still an active volcano.

The U.S. also sent out an expedition at this time. It was led by Lt. Charles Wilkes of the U.S. Navy. Wilkes was sent off with ships that were poorly equipped. In spite of this, he sighted and sailed along about 1500 miles of unknown coastline. It is now called Wilkes Land. When Wilkes returned home, he was not honored. The United States government did not even bother to have his reports published. It is interesting that Wilkes *was* honored in Europe, and awarded a gold medal in England.

In 1897, Adrien de Gerlache de Gomery led an expedition from Belgium. His ship was the *Belgica*. When they landed on the rocky coast, the crew's naturalist, a Rumanian named Racovitza, discovered little black insects under some rocks. They were like flies without wings, only ¼ of an inch (about 6 mm.) long. These were the first creatures to be found living right on the mainland. He named them *Belgica antarctica*.

De Gerlache and some of his men slept in a tent on shore for six nights. This was the first time anyone had stayed overnight in Antarctica.

Four years later, a scientific expedition came from Sweden. Its commander was a geologist named Otto Nordenskjold. On board their ship, the *Antarctic*, was also a botanist, and other experts on water, weather, magnetism and astronomy.

Anchoring near an island, they first explored what was in the sea. They threw out nets which went 500 feet down (about 150 meters). This is what Nordenskjold wrote in his notes:

> "Every time the net came up it was almost literally filled with a wonderfully rich mass of living organisms... it was not only the number of specimens which amazed us, but their variety, size and peculiar appearance."

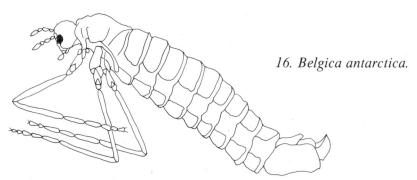

16. Belgica antarctica.

17. Nordenskjold found leaf fossils which showed that Antarctica was once warm and green.

We know today that the southern ocean is more filled with living things than any other ocean in the world. Nordenskjold's expedition was the first to discover this.

On land, Nordenskjold made an even more exciting discovery. As a geologist, he was an expert on rocks. As he was examining some Antarctic rocks, he found imprinted in them fossils of leaves from pine, beech and redwood trees. This showed that Antarctica had not always been a frozen land where nothing could grow.

Later on, other explorers discovered fossils of fern, palm and fig leaves—all of which usually grow in warm climates. They found petrified logs and coal, too. This showed that Antarctica was once warm and green.

The Ice Age came to Antarctica between 11 and 14 million years ago. The fossil leaves were from before that time. No one has yet discovered anything to prove that any large land mammals ever lived in Antarctica, although they have found fossils of amphibians that were as large as sheep.

Why did Antarctica get so much colder?

Here is one theory that many scientists believe. More than 200 million years ago, South America, Africa, India, Australia and Antarctica were not separate continents. Instead, they were all connected, forming one very large land mass, which scientists call GONDWANALAND.

About 135 million years ago, they began to split apart. Slowly, the continents moved away from each other. They were pushed by pressures that bubbled up from beneath the sea-bed. We call this moving apart "continental drift."

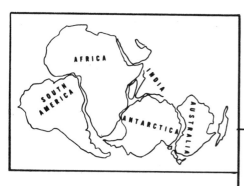

18. GODWANALAND, the "super-continent", about 135,000,000 years ago.

19. From 135,000,000 to 40,000,000 years ago.

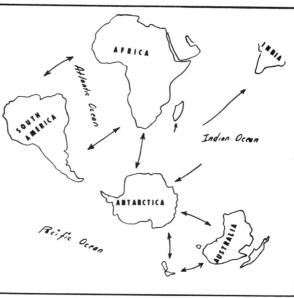

20. From about 40,000,000 years ago to the present.

Antarctica drifted south, to a colder part of the world, and that is why it is colder now than it used to be. Even today the continents are still "drifting."

Many men from different countries helped to discover Antarctica. Each voyage added a bit of knowledge. Some men left their names on the map of Antarctica: Davis Sea, the Ross Ice Shelf. Antarctic wildlife also bears their names: Wilson's storm petrel, Ross seal, Weddell seal.

No trip to Antarctica was easy. It called for courage and strength. Here are things that happened on two of these voyages.

The sea ice closed in on de Gerlache's ship, the *Belgica*. They were frozen in for 347 days. They were the first men who ever lived through a winter in Antarctica.

They lived on the ship. They had fuel for heat, and were able to eat seal and penguin meat. But what they suffered from most was the long Antarctic nights. For more than two months, they did not see the sun. Two of the men went mad.

They all looked forward to the end of that winter. But when spring came, they saw that the ice that surrounded them was still not breaking up. They finally freed the ship by sawing a 1½ mile canal (about 2 km) through the three-foot thick (about 1 meter) ice.

Sir Ernest Shackleton of Ireland sailed to Antarctica in 1914. He wanted to cross the entire continent by sledge. About 100 miles offshore (about 160 km), his ship was also frozen in. The men went out onto the ice with saws and picks. But they could not cut the ship free. Finally the *Endurance* was totally crushed by the sea ice.

Shackleton and the 27 crewmen took to the ice. They drifted on large ice floes. They had taken longboats off the *Endurance*. When they reached open water, they rowed and sailed for 60 hours through seas filled with icebergs and killer whales. At last they reached Elephant Island.

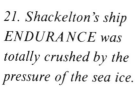

21. Shackelton's ship ENDURANCE was totally crushed by the pressure of the sea ice.

24

22. They made their way across the open water.

Most of the crew camped here. Then Shackleton and five others set out for help in a 20-foot (about 6 meters) longboat. They sailed 800 miles (about 1280 km). After 16 days, they reached a Norwegian whaling station on South Georgia Island.

Shackleton inspired his men. They had great faith in him. The men left on Elephant Island never doubted that he would come back with help. And he did.

23. They shove off from Elephant Island, to sail 800 miles for help.

During these early years of discovery, there was one thing no one had done. No one had ever set foot on the South Pole.

In October, 1911, two explorers started out. Each one wanted to be the first to reach the South Pole. One expedition ended in victory. The other ended in death.

Roald Amundsen was a Norwegian explorer. He headed for the Pole with five men and 52 huskies.

Captain Robert Falcon Scott was a British naval officer. Instead of huskies, he took Mongolian ponies to pull the sledges. He also had motorized sledges.

The summer before, they had placed supply depots along the first part of the way to the Pole. Now they followed these routes.

They started from different places on the coast, Scott setting out a few days after Amundsen. Amundsen had 870 miles to go (about 1400 km). Scott's route was 60 miles or about 96 km longer.

24. Roald Amundsen headed for the Pole with 5 men and 52 huskies.

25. Dr. Wilson and Nobby—one of the Mongolian ponies used on the Scott Expedition.

It was a trip no one had ever made before. There were icy mountains to climb. There were crevasses to watch out for—great deep cracks in the ice that are hidden under the snow.

Things went wrong for Scott from the start. The motorized sledges broke down and had to be dumped. The ponies could not stand the cold. They got weaker and weaker. One by one, they had to be shot.

A "support group" of men, huskies and supplies accompanied Scott until he was 170 miles from the Pole (about 272 km). Then, according to plan, the support group turned back. Only Scott and four other men headed for the Pole. The men, on skis, had to pull sledge-loads of supplies. It exhausted them. Some days they moved ahead only a few miles.

Meanwhile, Amundsen's group, using huskies, often traveled 30 miles in one day (about 48 km.).

Then, along the way, Amundsen had 24 of his dogs shot. It was a sad thing to have to do. But this provided fresh meat for the remaining huskies and the men. Amundsen grieved as he heard the shots ring out. But this had been part of his plan. And he felt it was essential for his success.

On December 14th, 1911, Amundsen, five other men and the 24 remaining huskies reached the South Pole. They stood at a place on earth where no one had ever stood before. They planted the Norwegian flag, and claimed the Pole for Norway. They camped there for three days. Then they started back. On January 25th, they reached their home base.

26. An overnight camp on Amundsen's expedition.

27. Scott's TERRA NOVA held in by pack ice.

A month later, Captain Scott and four other men—Bowers, Evans, Oates and Wilson—arrived at the Pole. But they never made it all the way back. First Oates and Evans died. Later, on March 31, Scott, Bowers and Wilson died in their sleeping bags, of exhaustion, hunger and cold. Scott's diary was found lying beside him. He had written: "We are getting weaker. The end cannot be far."

The rescue party found them frozen in their tent. They were only about eleven miles (about 17½ km) away from one of their return food depots.

28. Should Scott have used his huskies all the way to the Pole?

Eighteen years later, the South Pole was reached in a different way. Admiral Richard Byrd flew over it. (Don't you think *Byrd* is a perfect name for the first man to *fly* over the South Pole?)

Byrd was an American from Virginia. In 1929, he and three other men took off from the Antarctic coast in a small three-engine plane. Byrd was the navigator. There was also a radio man, a photographer and a pilot.

As they were flying through a valley, they found they could not climb high enough to get over the mountain that closed in the far end of the valley. And the pass was so narrow, they could not turn around. There was only one thing to do. They had to dump some weight. Then they could gain altitude, and try to get over the mountain.

If they dumped gas, they would not have enough fuel to get as far as the Pole. If they dumped food, they could not survive if they had to make an emergency landing.

They discussed it, and all four men agreed. They opened the trap door, and dropped out 200 pounds of food (about 90 kilograms.)

The plane climbed a little, but still not enough. They threw out more food. The plane rose just enough to clear the enclosed end of the valley by a few hundred feet.

They circled the Pole, but did not land. They took aerial photographs and dropped British, Norwegian and American flags. Then they headed back to the base. The entire flight took 18 hours.

29. Byrd checks his position with a sun compass.

30. Byrd with his dog, Igloo.

31. A "Byrd's-Eye-View" of Antarctica. Mt. Erebus is at upper right.

For Byrd, the Pole seemed almost a disappointment. He wrote: "The Pole lies in the center of a limitless plain. And that is almost all there is to say about it. It is the effort of getting there that counts."

Byrd made valuable surveys. From the air, he was able to chart the coastlines and mountains. It was now possible to have an over-all picture of the great white continent. Byrd gave us a bird's-eye-view of Antarctica.

Who Lives in Antarctica?

Penguins and seals live there. Some seabirds and insects live there, too.

It is almost a miracle of nature that these creatures can survive in Antarctica. But they can. They can live there because they get their food from the sea—for unlike the land, the Antarctic sea is rich with life. They dive for fish, squid and other sea life.

One important form of sea life is krill. *Krill* is the name for masses of small red shrimplike creatures that drift through the water. Krill is one kind of *plankton,* which is the name for many different small forms of life that drift in the ocean.

Whales swim thousands of miles from other oceans to visit the Antarctic seas, where they fatten themselves up on krill. A blue whale can eat 3 tons of krill every day.

Penguins and seals also eat krill. If you see a red stain on a penguin's front, it shows he has been eating krill.

33. Krill clump together so closely that between 2,000 and 8,000 have been counted in one cubic foot of water.

No trees grow in Antarctica. So, birds make their nests in other places. Some make nest-holes in the ground in ice-free spots near the shore. Others nest in cracks on high rocky cliffs.

The wandering albatross is one of the largest birds in the world. Its wingspread is about 11 feet, or more than 3 meters. It flies in great circles over the sea, gliding on the wind.

There are also birds called petrels. Some types are almost as large as the albatross. Others are small.

The Snow petrel, white as snow except for its jet black bill and·eyes, lives all year in the Antarctic. Other petrels fly north in winter. After nesting in Antarctica, Wilson's storm petrels are sometimes seen in New York harbor.

The skua is a large, gull-like bird. It eats penguin eggs and young penguins, as well as fish and krill from the sea.

34. Snow petrel

35. The skua is a large, gull-like bird.

36. An Adélie penguin...
has flippers instead of wings.

Penguins and Seals

Look at the penguin. It is a bird, but it doesn't fly. It has flippers instead of wings.

Look at the seal. It has flippers instead of legs.

Having flippers suits them both for their life in the sea. It makes them good swimmers, which is important, for they spend most of their lives in the sea.

How else are they alike?

37. A Weddell seal and her pup... have flippers instead of legs.

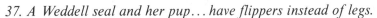

38. An Adélie penguin "porpoising".

They are both fat. Their fat also suits them for their life in the cold Antarctic. It acts as insulation; it keeps their body heat in.

The penguin has fatty tissue under its skin, and its feathers are like a warm coat, too. They are short and close-fitting feathers. They give out an oily substance which also helps to keep in body heat.

The seal, too, has fatty tissue called blubber under its skin. This keeps it warm. Its hair has an oily substance in it, too.

39. Two Weddell seals. Being fat helps keep them warm.

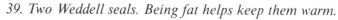

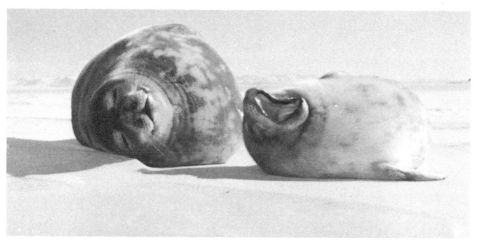

40. Weddell seals.
Being in the water a lot
also helps keep them warm.

Being in the water a lot also helps keep seals and penguins warm. Because even when the temperature is much colder on land, the Antarctic water stays at about a steady 28°F. (about –2°C.)

There is a kind of seal in Antarctica called the leopard seal. A leopard seal has a very big mouth and teeth and throat. And it eats penguins.

It can swim faster than a penguin can. But the penguin can zig-zag, and dodge. So, if the penguin has a good head start, it can get away. Then, it will swim fast at an upward angle, pop out of the water six feet into the air, and land on the ice, where it is safe.

41. A leopard seal has big teeth... and it eats penguins.

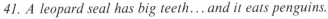

42. Three Adélie penguins popping up out of the water.

Sometimes you see a leopard seal lying up on the ice, with penguins walking nearby. Does that surprise you? Leopard seals hunt penguins in the water. But they will usually not attack them on land. The penguins know this.

On the whole great white Antarctic continent, the only creatures that really live on the land are insects. Midges and mites live in patches of moss that grow on rocky mountainsides, in spots that are sheltered from the wind.

The insect eggs stay frozen all winter. They thaw out and hatch the next year. The moss they live in often grows near bird rookeries, where it is fertilized by the bird excrement—called "guano."

Ticks and lice also live on the sea birds, penguins and seals.

The largest land-living creature on the entire continent is the wingless fly, *Belgica antarctica,* only about ¼ of an inch (6 mm.) long. (See picture on page 20.)

More About Penguins

Sometimes people say the penguin is a funny-looking creature. It doesn't look like most other birds—but does that make it funny?

The largest kind of penguin is the emperor penguin. They are almost 4 feet tall (about 110 cm.) and weigh between 70 and 80 pounds (31 to 36 kg) and they are strong. If the emperor penguin hits you with a flipper, it can break your arm.

In March, the beginning of the Antarctic autumn, the emperor penguins come in from the sea. They waddle over the ice to last year's breeding ground. This place is called the rookery. Sometimes thousands of them gather together. There, the males and females mate.

43. Emperor penguins are almost 4 feet tall.

39

44. Penguins walk long distance over the ice.

A month later, the female lays a big egg, weighing about 1 pound (about ½ a kg). She does not build a nest. She lays the egg on her feet, as she stands on the ice. Then she passes the egg to the father penguin. She does this very carefully, because if the egg cracks or freezes, no chick will hatch.

Now the mother penguin leaves the rookery. She walks back across the ice to the sea, so she can get food. It is a longer walk than it was before, because more ice has formed over the sea. Now the water's edge could be as far as 50 miles (about 90 km) away.

When she gets to the sea, she fills up on fish and squid and krill. Then she walks back to the rookery.

She has been gone about two months. All that time, the father penguin has been carefully holding the egg on his feet, keeping it covered and warm under a special fold of

45. Sometimes, instead of walking, they lie on their chests, and push themselves along with their flippers.

fat on his body. He has turned the egg around from time to time, so that all parts of it get his body heat.

It is now the freezing dark Antarctic winter. There are blizzards and hundred-mile-an-hour winds. Still, the penguin fathers stand, huddled together, shoulders touching, sharing their body heat and guarding their eggs. They change positions in the group once in a while, so that no one penguin stays out at the colder, exposed edge of the group for too long.

When the mothers return, the eggs are just about ready to hatch. Carefully, each father passes the egg back to the mother penguin. Now it is the father's turn to walk to the sea for food. He has not eaten for about three months. He has been living off reserve fat, and has lost about 40% of his body weight.

When the chick hatches out of the egg, it sits where it is warm, on its mother's feet. She feeds it regurgitated food that she brings up from her stomach.

The chick is a fluffy gray thing. Soon it is able to go out into the cold world. Still, the mother must not look away for even a minute. If the chick wanders too far off, a skua might swoop down and eat it.

Now the father penguins begin to return, and father and mother take turns feeding their chick. The chick grows larger and stronger. Soon it can stay with a group of other chicks. They are guarded by grown-up penguins who are not their mothers and fathers. Now the mothers and fathers can go looking for food together.

46. This penguin is in a safe, warm place—on its father's feet, under his special fold of fat. The father can even walk with the chick on his feet.

In about five months, the young penguins lose their soft gray baby covering, and grow adult feathers. Then all the penguins leave the rookery, and walk to the sea. Once again, the water's edge is not so far away. For the weather has been getting warmer, and the sea ice has begun to break up.

This is an important learning time for the young ones. They practice swimming, diving and catching fish.

At this time, the leopard seals lie in wait in the water. Sometimes, as a young penguin jumps into the water for the very first time, it is grabbed and eaten. Only one out of four chicks lives to become a grown-up penguin.

In December, which is mid-summer, big pieces break off from the edge of the sea ice. The penguins sit on these ice floes, and drift up to northern waters. There they swim and fish, and fatten up. In autumn, they will swim back to Antarctica, walk to their rookery, and the whole cycle begins again, as it has for millions of years.

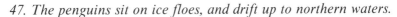

47. The penguins sit on ice floes, and drift up to northern waters.

A.

B.

E.

I.

F.

J.

C.

D.

G.

H.

48.

A. Adélie penguins were so named by Admiral D'Urville, for his wife, Adélie.

B. It is courting season at the rookery.

C. They make nests out of stones, which they gather.

D. The male is putting another stone on the nest rim.

E. Keeping the egg warm.

F. The chick has hatched.

G. The chick is guarded by mother and father.

H. The chick gets bigger.

I. The skua is the penguin's enemy.

J. An unwelcome visitor. A skua eats a chick that has died.

49. Chinstrap penguin.
Can you see how it got this name?

Adélie penguins are around 2 feet (about 60 cm tall), and weigh about 10 pounds (4½ kg). They make nests out of stones. The father and mother Adélies share the job of guarding the eggs and feeding the chicks.

There are 17 different species of penguins. Four of these—emperor, Adélie, chinstrap and gentoo—breed on the Antarctic mainland. Most of the others live on rocky islands in the Antarctic Ocean.

There have been penguins on earth for about 50 million years. It is possible that long ago, they were once able to fly. But scientists do not know this for sure.

50. *McMurdo Station, a U. S. base. Mt. Erebus in the background.*

What Is Antarctica's Future?

1957 was called the International Geophysical Year. Scientists from all over the world worked together to learn more about the world, and shared their knowledge with each other.

In Antarctica, about 10,000 men from different countries worked at sixty separate bases. They studied gravity and magnetism. They studied the layers of the snow. They studied temperature, and wind, and atmospheric pressure. They studied the ice sheet, and how fast it was moving.

*51. These women scientists collect soil and water samples.
(They crouch under the air blast of a departing helicopter.)*

More and more, they learned how important Antarctica
is. They found that what happens in far-off Antarctica
affects living things all over the rest of the world.

They found that nutrients from Antarctic waters drift
all the way up to northern oceans where they help to feed
much of the sea life there.

We know that Antarctic currents cool all the world's
oceans. And we know the Antarctic ice sheet contains
more than 90% of the world's water supply.

The cooperative scientific work in Antarctica did not
end when the International Geophysical Year was over.
The work has gone on and the bases kept open.

52. U.S. biologist studies plankton samples.

In recent years, scientists have discovered something that worries them. They have found DDT and other poisonous man-made chemicals in the body tissues of seals, penguins and skuas, and also in the Antarctic snow. Not even far-off Antarctica can escape pollution.

How do the poisons get there?

They could have blown in on the air, and dropped onto the ice sheet. They could have drifted down in ocean currents. Or they could have been brought down by migrating birds who had eaten seeds sprayed with DDT in the north.

How will this affect us? Does it mean that these poisons in the Antarctic snow will be recycled and come back up to us again in the world's water supply?

Scientists are trying to answer these questions. They are also continuing to measure the level of these poisons in Antarctica, to see if it increases.

In the summer of 1976-77, scientists worked on a special project: to drill a hole through the Ross Ice Shelf. Men from ten different countries—Great Britain, Japan, Denmark, Australia, Norway, the Soviet Union, New Zealand, West Germany, Switzerland and the United States—worked together on this project.

Why make a hole through the ice shelf?

First, they wanted to study creatures that live beneath the shelf, and learn about forms of life that can exist in total darkness.

53. Scientific research vessel HERO. It is used to collect samples of Antarctica sea life.

54. Drilling rig on the Ross Ice Shelf.

They were also eager to study the "bottom water." Bottom water originates under the shelf. It is water which flows close to the ocean bottom, then comes up to mingle with the rest of the ocean water. This bottom water is the richest water in the world. It is filled with nutrients that feed sea life in waters all over the rest of the world.

Scientists also know that the world's oceans are rising around 1/25th of an inch (about 1 mm a year). This is about four inches (about 100 mm) in 100 years. That may not sound like much. But suppose it keeps rising for thousands of years? What would happen to all the cities built on seacoasts?

Scientists feel the oceans are rising because of something happening beneath the shelf. But what? They hope to find out.

The ice where they began to drill is about 1,375 feet (419 meters) thick. Before they could get all the way through, the hole froze and closed up.

The following year, they succeeded. In December, 1977, using a jet of flame, they drilled a 12-inch hole (about 30 cm) through the ice. Cameras were lowered to the bottom. Small fish swam into view. On the sea bottom, another 780 feet (about 237 meters) down, photographs showed trails, burrows and other signs of life. The scientists also drew up rock samples and sediment, and cut ice cores from different levels. The nitrogen and other substances found locked in various layers of the ice can give us information about the climate of about 100,000 years ago.

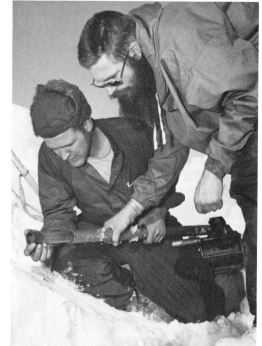

55. Samples of animal life are suspended in this core of ice taken from the Ross Ice Shelf.

Who Owns Antarctica?

In the past, when an explorer discovered a new place, he would claim it for his country. It would then "belong" to that country.

Antarctica is one place where things have not worked out that way.

Seven different countries have made claims there. But right now, these countries have agreed to share in the use of all Antarctica. And no part of Antarctica belongs to any particular country. Whatever happens in Antarctica affects all of the rest of the world, and so it is not and should not be owned or controlled by any one nation. It is protected by an agreement called the Antarctic Treaty.

This is what the Antarctic Treaty says:

1. Antarctica can be used for peaceful purposes only.
2. No country is allowed to build military bases there.
3. No country is allowed to test nuclear weapons there.
4. No country is allowed to dump nuclear wastes there.
5. Scientists from all lands will continue to investigate Antarctica. Whatever they learn, they will share with one another.
6. All national claims to Antarctica have been set aside, at least for the present.

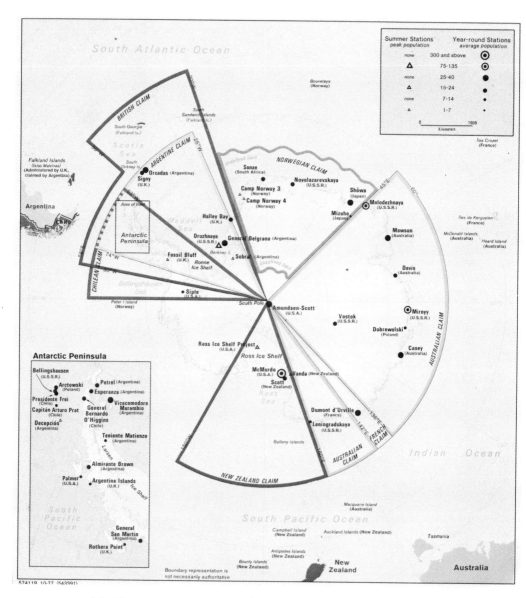

56. *The seven countries with claims have agreed to share in the use of Antarctica.*

This agreement was signed in 1959 by the twelve countries that first set up scientific bases in Antarctica: Argentina, Australia, Belgium, Chile, France, Japan, New Zealand, Norway, South Africa, the Soviet Union, the United States, and Great Britain. Later on, more countries signed the agreement. These were Czechoslovakia, Denmark, Poland, Rumania, the Netherlands, West Germany and Brazil.

Any member nation has the right to inspect any of the others' bases if it suspects that Treaty rules are being broken.

The Treaty will last for at least thirty years. In 1991, the member nations will then decide whether they want to make changes in it, or keep the agreement as it is.

There are also rules to protect the seals and penguins:

No one is allowed to land a plane near large groups of seals or penguins.

No guns, tractors or explosives may be used near them.

No dogs are allowed to run loose.

57. Antarctic Treaty delegates, and the flags of the treaty nations.

58. *Weddell seal pup.*

There has been a rule banning the killing of seals on the Antarctic continent except for a few which are used to feed huskies at the bases. But seals on the pack-ice were not so protected, since the pack-ice is technically not part of the continent.

In the early days of seal-hunting, seals were almost totally wiped out in some places by commercial seal hunters. To prevent any danger of over-hunting on the pack-ice, a new set of rules was drawn up in 1972, called The Convention for the Conservation of Antarctic Seals.

59. *Crabeater seals drift along on an ice floe.*

60. Weddell seal pup near its mother.

It states that only a certain limited number of seals are permitted to be killed each year. Since the Ross Seal is rare, none of them are to be killed.

New questions about Antarctica keep coming up, and new decisions have to be made every once in a while by the treaty nations. In March, 1978, they had a meeting in Australia to discuss krill. Because krill is rich in protein, some countries have begun to gather it from Antarctic waters, and make it into a food product for people to eat. But we know how vital krill is in the food chain as a main food for seals, penguins, squid, whales and other forms of sea life. What would happen if too much krill were to be removed from the sea? To prevent that, the treaty nations decided at their meeting to set a limit on the amount of krill that may be harvested.

Whales

One Antarctic creature *not* protected by the Antarctic treaty is the whale. Millions of whales have been killed in Antarctic waters.

In 1946, the International Whaling Commission (the IWC) was formed to make rules about whale-hunting. It meets each year, and sets limits on the number of whales allowed to be killed in the coming year.

But the limits have not been strict enough. Because of this, various species of whales may soon become extinct. The blue whale is in such danger. Although the blue whale is now "protected", and no one is allowed to kill them, this protection may have come too late. The blue whale—the largest mammal ever to live—has been so over-hunted in the past, that the number of them left is estimated to be very low. Some scientists believe that even now there are too few left to be able to build up their numbers again.

At a meeting in Stockholm, Sweden, in 1972, scientists from all over the world voted that it would be best if all whale-killing were stopped for a ten-year period. But the IWC would not agree to this. The two main whale-hunting countries are Japan and Russia. From the whales, they manufacture shoe polish, cosmetics, linoleum, shaving cream, machine oil and pet food. All of these products could be made of other ingredients.

In 1977, more than 25,000 whales were killed.

61. This species of whale is "Orca"—sometimes called the Killer Whale.

62. Orca does some acrobatics in icy Antarctic waters.

63. Are too many whales being killed?

64. Cutting up a whale.

Is There Any Way Man Can "Use" Antarctica?

When a man makes a discovery, people generally ask how it can be used.

Antarctica is mostly ice.

How can we use ice?

Admiral Byrd said perhaps we should use Antarctica as a deep freeze, and store extra food there until we need it.

Some scientists say we might try to float up icebergs to parts of the world where there is a water shortage.

There may be offshore oil in Antarctic seas. We also know that there is uranium in its mountains. But in this land "peskered with ice," it might take so much energy to get at it, that it would not, in the end, be worthwhile. There is also the danger that mining or deep-sea drilling in Antarctica might do such bad damage and cause such dangerous pollution to the seas and the ice sheet—so vital to the world's water supply—that it would be foolish to risk even trying it.

The Antarctic Treaty nations are aware of these problems. In 1977, they met in London and voted to ban Antarctic mining and offshore oil drilling for now.

The Antarctic Treaty was created in the spirit of world cooperation. And it will give us time to think carefully about these things before definite decisions are made.

65

Antarctica, although it is millions of years old, is, in a way, a fresh new world to mankind. Maybe we will decide that the best way to "use" Antarctica is not to use it at all.

PICTURE CREDITS *(Photographs are indicated by number.)*

American Geographical Society, New York: 10, 17, 63, 64
Library of Congress: cover, 25, 27, 28 (*by H.G. Ponting*), title page,
    7, 21-23, 26
National Maritime Museum, London: 12 (*lithograph by Louis Le
    Breton*), 14 (*painting by J.R. Wildman*)
National Science Foundation: 2, 15, 18-20, 34, 35,
        38, 41, 42 (*photo by William R. Curtsinger*), 49, 56,
        back cover (*top right, bottom left, bottom right*)
Radio Times Hulton Picture Library, London: 9
Royal Norwegian Embassy, London: 24
Scott Polar Research Institute, Cambridge, England: 11
United States Navy: 1, 3, 4, 6, 29-33, 36, 37, 39, 40, 43-47, 48A-I, 50-52,
        53 (*photo by William R. Curtsinger*), 54, 55, 57-62, 65,
        back cover (*top left, center*)
United States State Department, Office of the Geographer: 8, 13
Drawings by Elizabeth Weiss: 5, 16

BIBLIOGRAPHY

ANTARCTICA: The Last Continent by Ian Cameron. Little, Brown
    and Company, Boston, Mass., 1974. (*Book originally designed
    and produced by George Rainbord Ltd., Marble Arch House, London.*)
THE ANTARCTIC by H.G.R. King. Arco Publishing Company, New
    York, 1969.
THIS IS ANTARCTICA by Joseph M. Dukert. Coward-McCann, New
    York, 1965.
AUDUBON MAGAZINE. March, 1973. Volume 75 Number 2.
FROZEN FUTURE. Edited by Richard S. Lewis and Philip M. Smith.
    Quadrangle Books, Inc., A New York Times Company, New York, 1973.
90 SOUTH by Paul Siple. G.P. Putnam's Sons, New York, 1959.
THROUGH THE FROZEN FRONTIER by Rear Admiral George J. Dufek,
    USN. Harcourt, Brace and Company, New York, 1959.
SCOTT'S LAST VOYAGE. Edited by Ann Savours. Introduction by
    Sir Peter Scott. London, Sidgwich and Jackson. 1974. Praeger
    Publishers, Inc., New York, 1975.
CAPTAIN SCOTT AND THE ANTARCTIC TRAGEDY by Peter Brent.
    Saturday Review Press, New York, and George Weidenfeld and
    Nicolson, Ltd., 11 St John's Hill, London, 1974.
SOUTH! by Sir Ernest Shackleton. Macmillan Company, New York, 1920.
ENDURANCE by Alfred Lansing. McGraw-Hill Book Company, Inc.,
    New York, 1959.
A CONTINENT FOR SCIENCE by Richard S. Lewis. Forward by
    Thomas O. Jones. National Science Foundation. The Viking Press, Inc.
    New York, 1965.
MAMMALS OF THE WORLD Third Edition. Volume 2. By Ernest
    P. Walker. The Johns Hopkins University Press, Baltimore, Md., 1975.

INDEX